MOVING TOWARD RESTORATION

A Journey with the God Who Sees Me

Angie M Barnes

ISBN: 979-8-218-93955-7

Contact Information:
lifelonglearningfoundation2023@gmail.com

First Edition

Table of Contents

Dedication

I dedicate this journey to my son, who has been my "stone" here on earth. He gives me the courage to keep going and the honesty to tell me when I'm messing up. With God leading me and my family beside me, I know that this is just Part One of the restoration. The best is yet to come.

Introduction:
The Master Architect of the Pivot

We all start out with a plan. Whether you are heading off to college or simply mapping out the next five years of your life, you likely have a vision that feels magnificent. When people ask, "What do you want to be when you grow up?" we usually have an answer locked and loaded. We convinced ourselves that we have it all figured out, and we certainly don't want anything—or anyone—interrupting the flow. We think we're doing it all right. Oh boy, do we think we're doing it right.

But there is a profound difference between Chronos—our chronological, planned-out human time—and Kairos, which is God's appointed, opportune moment. This book is an invitation to look at your life through a different lens. It's about the "Daily Move"—the understanding that while we are busy trying to get from point A to point B, God is often orchestrating a pivot that leads us toward a purpose we never could have engineered ourselves. In this chapter, I want to share how my own "perfect" plans for a medical career were interrupted by a divine calling that I didn't even recognize at the time.

The Blueprint of a "Good Girl"

Growing up, my life was defined by a certain kind of order. I was a "good girl." I did what my parents said, I listened to my teachers, and I made sure I was where I was supposed to be when I was supposed to be there. At the time, I wasn't necessarily thinking in terms of being a "child of God"; I was just being obedient to the adults in my life. I was focused on the daily grind of building self-esteem and trying to be a positive influence.

Looking back, it's easy to see where I was off track, but in the moment, I was just trying to be the person everyone else expected me to be. However, God was already planting seeds. He uses our natural interests to spark our ultimate purpose. For me, that spark was two-fold: children and science.

My grandmother was the giant in my world. She was the one holding everything together, working a job she left for before I woke up and returned from before I got home, all while being the primary caretaker for every child in the family. I wanted to be just like her—surrounded by children, watching over them, being the heart of the home.

The Spark of Discovery

While my heart was with the children, my mind was captured by the world around me. I had a teacher named Alberta Palmer who changed everything. She didn't just teach science; she lived it. She would have us lie in the middle of the schoolyard—which, in our Little House on the Prairie style life, was just the grass we walked on to get home—and look at the clouds. She taught me to see how the light affected everything. To this day, I am a proponent of The Light. I always want to be in it.

I didn't realize it then, but God was directing my steps through my education:

- **The Creative Call:** My teacher Mrs. Johnson had us write a short story. I thought it was just extra homework, but that story, "Something Creeping in the Night," was published in a county-wide book. It was my first "publication," and I didn't even care about it at the time.

- **The Scientific Foundation:** Mrs. Palmer used us as living experiments, showing how our pupils dilated in the light.

- **The Academic Drive:** I moved from elementary to junior high, where graduating ninth grade was a huge milestone—equivalent to a high school diploma in those days.

By the time I hit high school and sat in Hattie Tillman's Advanced Biology class, I knew my path. I wasn't going to be a "housewife" in the traditional sense; I was going to be a doctor. I was fascinated by bodily functions and chemistry. Everything came easy because I was interested, and when you're interested, you make yourself do well.

The Intersection of Purpose and Interruption

I followed the plan. I did well on the ACT. I was accepted into the Summer Science Program at Tougaloo College, a school known for churning out more Black doctors and professionals than almost anywhere else. When they offered me a full ride on the spot, I knew it was where I was supposed to be. The goal was clear: get the BS in Biology, which quickly turned to Chemistry because I hated memorizing plant stuff, as I called it, then head straight to medical school.

Then, God interrupted.

During my senior year, I became pregnant. Suddenly, the body I had studied so diligently in textbooks was doing things I didn't understand. I found myself calling my doctor every two seconds, confused and overwhelmed. It was in those moments of vulnerability that I had a realization: I am too much of a public servant. I realized that if I became a medical doctor, I would never be able to "turn it off." I wouldn't be able to ignore the calls; I would be consumed by the needs of others at the expense of my own child.

To many, this looked like a "U-turn" or a failure of the original plan. It looked like "out of order" living. But in reality, it was a divine pivot.

"God was saying: 'No, I have something deeper for you. I'm going to grant you the things I promised, but I'm going to do them My way, not your way.'"

Instead of the MCAT (Medical College Admission Test), I took the PCAT (Pharmacy College Admission Test). I moved into pharmacology and toxicology. Once again, God provided a full ride, pregnant and all, right in my hometown of Jackson, Mississippi. He kept me close to my support system while still honoring my love for science.

From the Lab to the Classroom

I spent six years in a grueling doctoral program. I was a minority in a space where I was often discriminated against, and I was the only Black student to ever come through that specific track. When my advisor became ill and the department tried to force me to start over from scratch, I reached a breaking point.

I was tired of people-pleasing. I was worried about what people would say if I "dropped out," but my sister gave me the perspective I needed: "You've been there six years. You've completed the task. You don't have to do this for them." My mother reminded me that no one could take the knowledge I had gained.

I walked out on a Wednesday and never went back.

I thought I was just getting a job to survive. I worked in a pharmacy; I traveled with my husband while he trained as a truck driver. Eventually, we landed in Atlanta for the 1996 Olympics. On a whim—or so I thought—I decided to take the teacher's exam. I had been substitute teaching and found that I actually liked it.

When the results came back with flying colors, the door to my true calling swung wide open. I realized that for my entire life—from babysitting at age nine to teaching graduate students during my own med school years—I had been an educator. God hadn't called me to be a medical doctor; He had called me to teach.

Standing Still in the Daily Move

When I look back at the journey from the schoolyard grass to the pharmacology lab to the classroom, I see that God's timing was always perfect. Even when the path felt like a fork in the road or a confusing detour, I was under an "assignment" I didn't fully understand.

If you find yourself in a season where your plans have been shattered or your path has been diverted, I have one piece of advice: Stand still.

- **Acknowledge the Pivot:** Don't fight the interruption; ask what it is teaching you.
- **Listen for the Voice:** We get so busy "doing" that we forget to "be." Stand still and know that He is God (Psalms 46:10).
- **Trust the Names:** When you don't know the way, remember who He is.
  - **El Roi:** The God who sees me.
  - **Jehovah Jireh:** The God who provides.

God sees you. He knows what you are going through before you even say a word. Your plans might have changed, but His purpose for you has never wavered. He is not just the Architect of your beginning; He is the Master of the Pivot.

Chapter 1:
The Chaplain I Didn't Know I Was

Looking back over the landscape of my life, I realize now that God was operating on a timeline I couldn't yet see. We often spend our years chasing titles, degrees, and professional accolades, thinking we are building a career, only to discover we were actually being shaped for a calling. For decades, I walked into classrooms, lecture halls, and medical suites believing my primary job was to educate. I didn't realize that every lesson plan I wrote and every student I mentored was quietly preparing me to step into a spiritual identity I never expected: the identity of a Chaplain.

The Root of the Nurturer

My journey toward this realization began long before I had a doctorate or a classroom of my own. It started with the simple act of caretaking. As far back as I can remember, I have been in contact with children, learning what it means to truly nurture another human being. To many, a teacher is someone who instructs you on how to read and write, but a nurturer teaches you how to care for yourself. They teach you how to navigate the world, how to sustain yourself, and how to survive.

Even as I pursued my own education, I didn't see that I was being trained for an even more in-depth level of nurturing. In college, I thought I was there to master science and pedagogy. I spent hours debating Christianity with professors who insisted that a chemistry book should be my Bible. I remember one specific "Invitation to Learning" class where the teacher was ready to fail me because I refused to abandon my belief in creationism for evolution. I was fighting for my faith in every paper I wrote.

I eventually sought advice from my pastor, the Reverend Dr. Nelson. He gave me a perspective that changed my life. He told me, "You're sitting here arguing over what you believe when it doesn't really matter to the grade. They have something you need right now. Stop the argument. You know what you believe." That was my first lesson in Time, Place, and Space. I learned that you carry your spiritual beliefs with you, but you must understand the context of where you are. I stopped the ego battle, got my "A," and moved on. I didn't know then that this ability to navigate different "spaces" would be the very thing that allowed me to bring the light of God into secular classrooms later in life.

From "Professor" to "Mama Dukes"

Whether I was teaching graduate-level medical students or high schoolers, I was always just "Angie" to myself. I was just doing the work. But my advisor saw something I didn't. He told me, "You're going to get this doctorate and you're going to end up teaching because I see it in you. You're too good with these students."

When I finally landed in the classroom, I felt it immediately: this is the fit. But the impact went far beyond the curriculum. My students started calling me "Mom" or "TeeTee." When I got to Kell High School, they called me "Mama Dukes." At first, I didn't understand the slang, but I eventually realized it was a term of deep reverence. They weren't just seeing an instructor; they were seeing a spiritual anchor.

I always felt it was necessary to pray, even when the setting made it a "conflict of interest." I would tell my students, "I'm walking out of the room for a moment. You guys do what you need to do, but I know when I get back, somebody better have said a prayer." They knew. They felt the requirement of the Spirit. Eventually, it became a standard at Kell—we opened every single day with prayer. It wasn't a ritual; it was a necessity. People started saying, "We need to make sure Angie is around so she can pray." I used to resist that, thinking, "That's not my role." I was wrong.

The Gift of Gab as a Spiritual Weapon

For my entire life, I have been told that I "talk too much." People called it the "gift of gab," and often, it was used as a put-down—a warning that my words would get me into trouble. But God never allowed me to shy away from it. I have come to realize that this trait is actually a vital tool for a prayer warrior.

I will talk to anyone, anywhere—even a fly on the wall! I've learned that when you offer a kind word to a stranger in Walmart, you open a door. A simple compliment about a dress leads to a life story, which leads to a moment of profound need. I have prayed for more people in the aisles of department stores than I can count. I've realized that:

- A kind word builds a bridge.
- A listening ear identifies the burden.
- A simple prayer provides the breakthrough.

That "gift of gab" allowed me to offer comfort to people I never knew needed it. I've had strangers tell me a hug was the best thing that happened to them all week. You never know how much people need to be seen until you take the time to talk to them.

Recognizing the Watchman

The "lightbulb moment" truly happened recently. My husband and son were starting a business, and while I was excited for them, I felt a little left out because it wasn't my "area." Then my son looked at me and said, "Mom, your role in this whole thing is going to be Chaplain. You'll be our Chaplain."

That touched me to the core. To be recognized as a prayer warrior by your own family is the highest honor. It coincided with a prayer conference I attended—one I didn't even realize was a prayer conference until I got there. It was there that I learned about "watch times." I discovered that my habit of waking up at 2:30 or 3:30 in the morning to talk to God wasn't just insomnia; it was my "watch." I had been a watchman on the wall for years without having the vocabulary to describe it.

God has spent years positioning me. He slowed me down, called my name through the car radio, and told me to "slow my roll" so I could finally hear Him clearly. He took my history as a student body president saying morning prayers over the intercom and wove it together with my career as an educator to create the Chaplain I am today.

I used to think being "qualified" meant having the right degree or being perfect. But the truth is, we are all qualified to lead others to the Light. I am no longer nervous about sharing the Gospel or opening a meeting with prayer. I've learned that if you just open the door with, "Let's pray," God will do the rest. I don't have all the answers for the people who bring me their problems, but I know the One who does. I've stopped fighting the label. I am a nurturer, a prayer warrior, and a Chaplain—not because I chose it, but because God prepared the space for me to step into.

Chapter 2:

The God Who Sees Me

For a long time, I moved through the world under the impression that I was simply a woman navigating a career in education and science. I saw my life in Chronos—as a sequence of degrees earned, lessons planned, and schedules kept. But looking back through the lens of Kairos, God's opportune timing, I realize that I was being shaped by a master architect. Long before I ever considered myself a "spiritual leader," God was planting the seeds of a chaplaincy I didn't even know I possessed.

This chapter is about how El Roi, the God who sees me, was working in the quiet, hidden spaces of my life—transforming my "gift of gab" into a tool for the Kingdom and revealing a calling that had been there all along.

The Nurturer in the Classroom

My journey into spiritual leadership didn't start at a pulpit; it started with the basic instinct to nurture. Long before I was teaching students how to read or write, I was a caretaker. To me, a nurturer is someone who teaches you how to care for yourself—how to navigate the world, how to be whole. I didn't realize that every step of my formal education was just deepening that well of nurturance.

Even in college, I was learning how to nurture people spiritually, though at the time, I mostly expressed it through debate. I remember fighting tooth and nail with a professor over evolution versus creationism. I was so young and headstrong; I refused to see any middle ground. My professor told me the chemistry book was my Bible, and I was offended to my core. It took my pastor, Dr. Nelson, to give me a perspective that changed my life. He told me, "You know what you believe. Stop the argument, get the grade, and move on."

That was a lesson in time, place, and space. I learned that I didn't have to win every argument to hold onto my light. This realization allowed me to enter the classroom not as a combatant, but as a light. When I eventually began teaching medical students and high schoolers, I found my "fit." I wasn't just a teacher; I was "Mom," "Tee-Tee," and "Mama Dukes." These weren't just nicknames; they were titles of reverence for a woman who saw them as more than just names on a roster.

The Rhythm of Prayer

In every school where I worked, prayer became my heartbeat. At Kell High School, we opened the doors with prayer every single day. Eventually, it got to the point where people would say, "We need to make sure Angie is around so she can pray us in."

I used to think that was just something I did, but looking back, the pattern was set much earlier. I had forgotten that as Student Body President in high school, it was my job to deliver the invocation over the intercom every morning. God was giving me a microphone for Him before I even knew what a "prayer warrior" was.

My mother taught me the practical power of faith early on. She'd say, "Once you've done all you can do, put your schoolwork under your pillow and pray over it. God will take up the rest." That became my life's rhythm:

- **Praying In:** Inviting God into the start of every meeting, class, and conversation.
- **Praying Out:** Sealing the work we did and releasing the outcome to Him.
- **The Watch:** Discovering that my natural wake-up times—2:30, 3:30, 4:30 AM—weren't just bouts of insomnia, but my "watch time" to stand in the gap for others.

The Gift of Gab

For my entire life, I was told I "talked too much." People called it the "gift of gab," and usually, it was meant as a put-down—a warning that my words would get me into trouble. But God never allowed me to shy away from it.

I've realized now that a prayer warrior needs the gift of gab. Because I'm willing to talk to a fly, I'm willing to talk to the stranger in the aisle at Walmart. I'll start with a simple, "That's a nice dress," and five minutes later, that person is pouring out their heart. I may not have twenty dollars to give them, but I have a prayer. And more often than not, that prayer and a hug are more valuable than any monetary gift.

> **Key Takeaway:** Your natural personality traits—the things people might have criticized you for—are often the very tools God wants to use for His glory.

When El Roi Reveals the Chaplain

The moment the "chaplain I didn't know I was" finally came into focus involved my son. When he and my husband were starting their business, he looked at me and said, "Mom, your role in this is going to be our Chaplain."

It touched me to the core. I had always felt unseen and, at times, unworthy. But El Roi, the God who sees me, knew I needed a human "package" to reflect that value back to me. He gave me a son who could see my spiritual worth and name it.

The final confirmation came at a prayer retreat. I received a desperate text for prayer and, out of habit, I tried to hand the responsibility off to a woman I considered a "real" prayer warrior. She looked at me and said, "No. If somebody asks you to pray, you stop and do it right then. Don't put it on the back burner."

Shortly after, a line sister called me in tears, needing me to go somewhere private to pray for her. In that moment, the light popped on. God wasn't asking me to find someone else to lead; He was telling me, "I chose you."

Seen and Sent

We are all qualified to lead others to Him because our worth isn't connected to dollars and cents—it's connected to our relationship with the Creator. For years, I was "studying at" life, putting my dreams under the pillow and hoping for the best. Today, I recognize that God has transitioned me from the classroom to the "watch," from a teacher of science to a witness of His Spirit. He saw me when I felt invisible, and now, I am standing in the light He provided, ready to see others the way He sees them.

Chapter 3:
Pivoting Without Panic

I had a plan. It was a good plan, a solid plan, the kind of plan you feel is set in stone because you've been chipping away at it since you were old enough to hold a book. From my earliest days, I was captivated by how the world worked. I had teachers who made science feel like a grand adventure and who looked at me and said, "You're brilliant; you can do anything."

But life rarely follows a straight line, especially when the world around you is trying to draw boundaries you never asked for. My journey has been defined by moments where the road I was on suddenly ended, forcing me to find a new path. I've learned that there is a profound difference between a detour and a dead end. When expectati xons break, you have a choice: you can freeze in fear, or you can learn the art of pivoting without panic.

The Early Shaping of Resilience

My first experience with a forced detour happened before I even understood what "prejudice" meant.

During the era of school segregation and the early days of integration, I was being bussed into white neighborhoods. I was just a little girl, but I was already a "problem" for a system that wasn't built for me.

In kindergarten, I was kicked out because a little white boy liked me and refused to go home unless he could ride with me. Suddenly, his preference became "my problem." It made me physically ill—the stress of being punished for things that weren't my fault, lead to the pediatrician having my parents remove me from kindergarten. That sound weird but true. Later, I was held back in second grade. At the time, I didn't understand why; my parents knew I was doing well, but the racial friction of that environment created a barrier I couldn't see.

Everything changed in third grade when our neighborhood schools opened. For the first time, I had Black teachers who truly cared about us. They didn't just follow a schedule; they sparked a fire. By fourth grade, we were changing classes for specialized subjects like science, math, and social studies. I was hooked. I remember watching a friend's pupils dilate in the sunlight and being absolutely fascinated. I wanted answers for everything.

That curiosity fueled my ambition. I decided then and there: I was going to be a doctor.

Lessons from the Early Years:

- **Your environment matters:** Moving to a supportive neighborhood school allowed my engagement to soar.
- **Excellence is the expectation:** My mom never paid us for grades. She told us, "Grades are your pay." It was our job to do well, and I took that job seriously.
- **Talent is multifaceted:** While I excelled in math and science, I discovered a hidden talent for writing, even winning awards in elementary school. Never box yourself into just one "thing."

Independence and the El Paso Summer

By the time I reached Tougaloo College on a full scholarship, my trajectory toward medical school seemed unstoppable. I was a chemistry major, diving deep into research. In the summer of 1988, I got a taste of true independence when I was granted a research internship at the University of Texas at El Paso.

El Paso was a revelation. It was the first time I was truly away from family, standing on my own two feet. I loved the independence of getting up, going to the lab, and conducting research on my own. I remember the fascination of watching people cross the Rio Grande daily to work—it was a world so much bigger than the one I had known in Mississippi.

In El Paso, I saw a future where I was a high-level researcher and a physician. I was "life-ing" at full speed, independent and capable. I liked that version of myself. But that lifestyle only lasted that summer. When I returned, I found out I was pregnant, and the "plan" hit a wall.

When the Plan Breaks: Pregnancy and Marriage

I'll be honest: finding out I was pregnant felt like a "halt." But contrary to what people might think, the pregnancy wasn't what stopped me from becoming a Medical Doctor. It was the pregnancy that revealed I didn't actually want to be an M.D.

As I felt the changes in my own body, I realized I was already a public servant at heart. I knew I'd be the kind of doctor who answered the phone at 3:00 AM and never sent a bill. My siblings used to joke, "You'll be the poorest doctor ever because you won't charge anyone." I realized then that I wanted the science without the business of clinical medicine. I pivoted—without panicking—into pharmacology and toxicology.

The bigger challenge, however, was marriage. Marriage was never in the plan. Even after the baby was born, I wasn't sure. It took six weeks of soul-searching and seeking God's guidance before I said "I do."

That was my true "blindsided" moment. Up until then, my decisions were mine. Suddenly, it wasn't just

"Angie" anymore. It was "we." I was trying to do things the "right" way—a word I now put in parentheses because what's "right" for society isn't always what's right for your spirit.

The Daily Pivot

People ask how I learned to pivot instead of panic. The truth is, I pivot every single day. Marriage, especially when you are navigating financial struggles or when you aren't perfectly "equally yoked" in the Word, is a constant exercise in redirection. There are moments of unease, moments where you feel like you're stuck at Point B and Point C is nowhere in sight.

In those moments, I've learned to be still.

Over the last few years, God has been using life's "halts" to get my attention. I broke my leg twice during COVID. I've had health scares where I literally stopped breathing. Each time, it was a reminder: Stop and listen. I have something to tell you.

How to Pivot Without Panic:

- **Trust the Restoration:** God has a way of bringing you back to your true self. Recently, I went on a prayer retreat that felt just like those independent days in El Paso—reminding me that I am still a traveler and a seeker.
- **Find Your Village:** Whether it was my aunt who owned the daycare or the intimate group of

women I study the Bible with now, you need people who don't see your faith as an insult or a "handicap."

- **Recognize the "Halt" as Preparation:** Being forced to sit down isn't a punishment; it's a classroom.

I am standing at the threshold of a whole new beginning. I've survived the detours of my youth, the unexpected turns of my education, and the trials of my marriage. I've learned that if you just hold on, God has more work for you to do. He isn't ready to take me out of here yet—He's just been teaching me so that I can teach others. We have to keep "keepin' on."

Chapter 4:

Just Wash Your Face

There is a specific kind of mountain you climb when your life shifts from the fast-paced world of career and ambition to the quiet, often painful reality of chronic illness. We spent the first part of this book laying a foundation of faith, but now we are entering a new season: the practice of daily movement.

When I talk about movement, I'm not talking about running marathons or hitting professional milestones. I'm talking about the holy victory of the smallest possible steps. To understand why something as simple as "just washing your face" became the core practical message of my life, I have to take you back to the moment the snowball started to roll—back to when I was a mother, a medical student, and a woman who didn't even realize she had stopped breathing.

The Snowball Effect: When Life Goes Sideways

You expect things to be great when you're at the "peak" of your life. For me, that was 1995. I was in my sixth year of medical school, I had a husband and three beautiful babies—ages five, four, and one. We were vacationing at Disney World, the happiest place on earth, but I was hiding a secret: I was incredibly ill.

As a mother, you feel like you have to keep going. That's just what we do. I had recently spent a week in the hospital with chronic bronchitis and asthma, and the doctors warned me that even a simple cold could land me back in a hospital bed. At Disney, I felt that cold coming on. I took a common over-the-counter medicine to hide my symptoms, but instead, I went into anaphylactic shock.

I spent another week in a Florida hospital, hovering in a space where I didn't even know I was in the world for a couple of days. That was the beginning of the snowball. When I finally made it back home, the hits kept coming. My doctoral advisor fell ill and passed away, and the university wanted me to start my six-year PhD process all over again.

I decided then and there that letters behind my name meant nothing compared to my health and my children. I walked away with a Master's degree instead of a Doctorate, and we relocated to Atlanta for my husband's job. I was chasing independence, working everywhere from the Olympics to a pharmacy, until God eventually made it clear that I had a calling I hadn't expected: teaching.

The Tug-of-War Between Calling and Comfort

I ended up in education by what felt like a fluke, but I now know it was a "God thing." I was teaching at the highest-ranking school in Georgia, and even when the CDC finally called me regarding a position that paid three times my salary, I couldn't take it. I didn't want to choose the money over the calling.

But while I was building a department from the ground up and coaching a dance team, my body was beginning to fail. The symptoms my mother had—the symptoms of Lupus—were starting to manifest in me. I knew just enough about medicine to be dangerous; I started self-medicating to stay in the game, to keep my independence, and to keep providing for my family.

Eventually, the "self-management" wasn't enough. I was having seizures. I was falling asleep in random places because the medication had taken over. I was a "Grace and Mercy sandwich"—just two slices of God's protection holding a mess of a life together. Finally, my doctor delivered the news that felt like a death sentence: "No more. You're out of work permanently."

Finding Purpose in the "Disabled" Space

Being pulled out of work took a massive toll on my psyche. My self-worth was tied to my paycheck and my independence. When I sat in a disability hearing and heard an attorney ask if I could wash dishes or be a short-order cook, I felt insulted. I had been to medical school! But then the truth hit me: I couldn't actually do those jobs. I couldn't hold a stable 9-to-5 because some days, I simply couldn't move.

It was during this time that God revealed His bigger plan. My sister became terminal with cancer. Because I was no longer working, I was able to move in and care for her for nearly two years.

My sister was the one who taught me the "Just Wash Your Face" philosophy. She was down to 68 pounds, yet she would get up every single day and make herself look "fly." She'd go to chemo looking gorgeous, cracking jokes, and radiating joy. She would look at me—upset about my disability and my lost house—and remind me: "You're still useful, just in a different way."

Before she passed, we closed on a small "HUD" home. I felt like I was settling, like I had lost my dignity because I wasn't in the big house we built from the ground up. But my sister helped me make the beds in every room, and when she was done, she looked at me and said, "Okay, I'm done." She passed away shortly after. She had spent her final strength making sure I had a home.

The Victory of the Smallest Step

There are days when your only job is to survive. I remember after breaking my legs during the pandemic, simply getting to the restroom was a victory. It would take me two hours to bathe myself using towels while sitting outside the tub, but I did it every single day.

Why? Because movement is progress.

When you are in a downward spiral of depression or physical pain, the enemy wants you to stay under the covers. He wants you to believe that if you can't do something "big," you shouldn't do anything at all. But I heard God's voice call my name in my garage one morning. He told me to "get it together" because I was feeling sorry for myself. He reminded me that I am still His servant, regardless of my physical limitations.

How to Practice Daily Movement

If you find yourself in a season where the mountain feels too high, remember these three things:

1. **Wash Your Face:** It sounds trivial, but it is a declaration of dignity. Comb your hair. Put on a clean shirt. As my grandmother used to say, "Pick your head up. What are you holding it down for?"

2. **Order Your Steps:** Start every morning with a simple prayer: "Order my steps, God. Help me discern Your voice from the enemy's."

3. **Accept God's Timing:** We mess up when we try to move on our own timeline. Progress isn't always a promotion; sometimes, progress is just waking up and saying "Thank You" for another day.

A New Beginning

Today, my joy comes from my eight "Grammy Award" grandchildren. They are my new reason to get up and be on point. I've realized that my independence doesn't come from a paycheck; it comes from the fact that God provides exactly what I need, exactly when I need it.

Every step forward, no matter how tiny, is a holy movement. Whether you are navigating a new diagnosis, a loss of career, or a season of grief, do not despise the small steps. Just get up, wash your face, and see what God has for you today.

Chapter 5:

Grammy Awards and New Beginnings

Life has a way of coming full circle, often in ways we never could have scripted for ourselves. When I think about this season of my life, the phrase that keeps surfacing is "a new beginning." But it isn't just any start; it is a divine second chance—a restoration. It is the opportunity to sit down, smell the roses, and blossom alongside my Grammy Awards.

For those who don't know, my "Grammys" are my grandchildren. The name started because I've always loved to sing. I sang my own children to sleep at night—even when they'd argue that I was getting the lyrics wrong—and I still call friends to sing to them on their birthdays. To me, a Grammy is the ultimate singing gift, but more importantly, an award is a blessing. It is a sign that God recognized me and said, "Here is something special." They are my gifts from God, each assigned a number based on their birth order to keep things straight, and each with their own custom rap song and dance.

The Beauty of the Do-Over

There was a time, not too long ago, when I felt lost. After my sister passed away, I struggled to find my purpose. I wasn't working in the same capacity, and I felt like I wasn't contributing to the world. But then came the babies.

When I was raising my own children, I was "lifing." I was in medical school, growing up right alongside them, and working tirelessly to provide a high-income household so they could have everything they wanted. I was focused on independence and provision, but in the process, I missed the quiet moments. I wasn't there as much as I wanted to be. My mother was the one who heard the secrets and stayed close because I was simply too busy.

Now, God has given me a "do-over." I am living in the sandwich generation, parenting "up" for my 81-year-old mother who lives with me, and parenting "down" for Grammy Award number one, my eleven-year-old granddaughter whom I acquired.

Just this past Monday, I was out shopping with her and her friend. They were looking for "berrr boxes" for their boyfriends, and I was exhausted, trying to keep up with them at 7:30 at night—well past my bedtime. My watch had died, and I was just trying to help them pick out gifts that weren't "cheesy." Later that night, I opened social media and a memory popped up: ten years ago to the day, I was out at a restaurant with that same child when she was just a year old.

I broke into tears. Ten years ago, I was reeling from the death of my sister, but God was already planting the seeds of a new beginning. He showed me that while I missed things with my first set of children, I wouldn't miss them this time. I'm living the life now—the shopping trips, the heart-to-hearts, the prayers before the school bus. It is a painful joy, a full-circle moment that makes me realize God had this plan in the making all along.

Ministry Within the Home

People often ask how to minister to their own families without it feeling forced or "mundane." I'll be honest: I went through a phase where I was hearing so much from God that I started writing scriptures on the walls of my house. My family thought I was losing my mind! I don't necessarily recommend the wall-writing, but I do recommend finding small, actionable ways to weave faith into the everyday.

- **The Lunchbox Liturgy:** I started packing lunches for everyone and writing scriptures or simple notes like "God loves you" on the sandwich bags or sticky notes. Even if they tell you they threw it away, believe me—they are reading it.
- **Visual Reminders:** Use wall art or "Daily Bread" books in common areas. "Be still and

know that I am God" placed over a doorway can capture a heart in a quiet moment.

- **The Power of the "Walk":** Eventually, I realized that my family needed to see my walk, not just hear my words. When I get up early to pray with my granddaughter, or when they see me committed to public service through my sorority, they notice.

In my household, I am the "Church Lady." My home is open to anyone who wants to study the Word, regardless of denomination. My family sees that commitment. They see me helping my "Sorors," taking them to the doctor, or involving my husband in service. When you move in faith, your family eventually moves with you.

Defining a True Legacy

When I think about the legacy I want to leave for my Grammy Awards, I think of my own grandmother. She had eleven children and dozens of grandchildren, yet she had a unique, special relationship with every single one of us. She was a powerhouse—an Eastern Star who drove around with Medgar Evers to register voters in Mississippi, a woman who built her own home to her exact specifications.

But her greatest legacy wasn't money; it was foundational wealth.

1. **Spiritual Guidance:** Knowing that God is first. If you put Him first, everything else follows.
2. **Service:** Staying active in the community and helping those who cannot help themselves.
3. **Presence:** Being the one who walks them to the bus, who cooks the Sunday morning meals, and who listens to the stories.

God has a way of "gracefully breaking you" to humble you, moving you away from the pursuit of titles and high incomes toward a life of gratitude and grace. I call myself a "grace and mercy sandwich" because I am tucked right between His favor and His protection every day.

My Grammy Awards are my reminder that life is worth living. They are the reason I want to keep learning, so I can teach them the "real"—not just math and science, but the truth of a history book called the Bible. I want them to know that they are part of a lineage of faith that cannot be shaken.

As you look at your own family, remember that it is never too late for a new beginning. Whether you are a parent, a grandparent, or a mentor, your "walk" is the loudest sermon you will ever preach. Focus on building a foundation of faith that your loved ones can stand on long after you are gone.

Chapter 6:
From Med School to Ministry in the Classroom

Life often feels like a series of forks in the road, and if we are honest, we spend a lot of time wondering if we took the right turn. For years, I looked back at my departure from medical research with a sense of unfulfillment, questioning if I had made a massive mistake or if I was simply failing to use the gifts God had given me. I had to learn that what we often perceive as a "wrong turn" is actually Divine Order. This chapter is about the transition from the sterile world of pharmacology to the vibrant, chaotic, and deeply spiritual world of the classroom. It is a story of how God closes doors not to punish us, but to save us from ourselves and redirect us toward a ministry we never saw coming.

The Fork in the Road: Leaving the Lab

Medical school and research were my ultimate dreams. I wanted to offer something tangible to the world, specifically in medical research, because I saw a desperate need for it within minority communities. In my studies at a historically black school, I learned the heartbreaking history of how minorities were often abused in the name of research—used for data that never actually benefited them. I wanted to fill that gap. I wanted to be the one to change that narrative.

I was "successful" by every worldly metric. I was at the University of Mississippi (Ole Miss) medical school—a place that, not long ago, wouldn't even allow Black students to walk through the doors. Not only was I there, but I was on a full ride; they were paying me to be there. I never called myself "smart"—I don't even know if I believe in that word—I just called it being willing to work hard.

However, the pivot came through a moment of profound loss. My advisor, a woman I loved dearly, fell ill with brain bleeds and eventually passed away. Before she died, she told me something that offended me at the time: "You're going to do all this, get this PhD, and you're going to be out teaching somewhere. What a waste."

I was shocked. I didn't care for teaching! But she saw the gift in me before I did. After she passed, I felt panicked and unsupported by the department chair. On a Wednesday, I walked out and never went back. At the time, I wondered if I was throwing it all away. Now, I realize that pivot was the grace of God covering my "mistake" and turning it into a mission.

The Accidental Ministry of Education

I ended up in Atlanta substitute teaching by what I thought was a fluke. I took the teacher's certification test, passed it on the first try, and was placed in a chemistry classroom. I didn't go to school for education; I didn't know the acronyms like IEP or BD. I was just an independent person trying to pay the bills.

But once I stepped into that room, I realized that teaching is a calling, not a learned skill. I had been a nurturer my whole life—taking care of my siblings since I was thirteen, balancing checkbooks, and "raising" cousins. In the classroom, I wasn't just teaching the periodic table; I was mothering. My students started calling me "Mom" and "Tee-Tee."

I soon saw the hand of God confirming this path in ways I couldn't ignore:

- **Financial Forgiveness:** I was worried about the $100,000 in loans/grants from my medical studies because I wasn't working in pharmacology. I wrote a letter explaining I was teaching chemistry, and the state forgave every single dime.

- **Exponential Impact:** In a lab, I would have published papers that only a few specialists would read. In the classroom, I was impacting hundreds of lives.

- **The Full Circle:** Today, one of my former students is my own doctor. Another followed my exact footsteps into pharmacology and toxicology. My "ministry" wasn't in the research itself; it was in the people I prepared to do the work.

Integrating Science and Spirit

People often say that science and God don't go together. I couldn't disagree more. When I was asked to open a new school as the Science Department Head, I built that department on a foundation of prayer. We were a family of like-minded scientists who prayed every day.

Even after my health forced me to pivot again—using my "pity party" days of illness to slow down and listen—God birthed a new season of education through my STEM children's books. These books, featuring my grandchildren (my "Grammy Awards"), allow me to make complex concepts like physics and chemistry simple enough for a two-year-old.

Ministry is not just talking about God; it is talking about things that affect someone's life over and over again. It is letting people see God through your walk, not just your words.

Trusting the Redirection

If you are facing a closed door or a forced "slow down" due to illness or circumstance, consider these truths about God's redirection:

1. **Closed Doors are Protection:** God often saves us from ourselves by closing off a path that would have led to burnout or unfulfillment.

2. **Illness as an Invitation:** Sometimes a "flare-up" or an injury is God saying, "Slow your roll. You can serve me better if you stop and listen."

3. **Preparation Takes Time:** Every delay is a season of preparation for the next step. You cannot rush the process of becoming who He needs you to be.

4. **Watch for the "Divine Flukes":** Look for the moments where things fall into place effortlessly—the passed test, the forgiven debt, the unexpected job offer. That is the "Divine Order" at work.

We must never give up hope. As long as we have hope, we have another day. Even when you feel you've taken the wrong fork in the road, God's mercy is big enough to navigate you back to His plan. Stop long enough to listen, and you will see His hands working in the redirection.

Chapter 7:

The Discernment to See the Connections

Life is often built on a foundation of second-guessing. Even now, at fifty-nine years old, I am still learning that my "type-A" personality—the part of me that desperately wants to "do it right"—is frequently the very thing that clouds my vision. We spend so much of our lives trying to figure out what the "right" move is, navigating a world filled with voices, expectations, and people we don't want to disappoint. Yet, I am discovering that true spiritual clarity doesn't come from perfect planning; it emerges through the discernment to see connections in the layered experiences God places before us.

Learning to walk by faith and not by sight requires a specific kind of spiritual sensitivity. It is the ability to distinguish between God's voice and the echo of my own anxieties or the demands of others. For a long time, I carried the label of "people pleaser" like an unwanted heavy coat. I tried to be the "rock" for everyone in my personal space, only to realize that in trying to please everyone, I was often neglecting the one voice that truly mattered. When you finally open your eyes and decide to be a "God-pleaser" instead, you realize that while all else should fall into place, the enemy often attacks through the people closest to you.

Discernment is the tool God gives us to navigate that pain. It is the quiet realization that even when we feel ostracized or misunderstood by our own inner circle, we are walking the path Jesus walked. He, too, was denied by His own. My journey through recent trials has taught me that God uses our "mess-ups," our moments of disobedience, and our divine appointments to weave a tapestry of purpose—if only we have the eyes to see the threads.

The School of Obedience

The power of discernment was made vibrantly clear to me during a recent retreat. I had initially thought the retreat was about "Purpose," but God had a different curriculum in mind: Prayer and Obedience.

Despite the financial hurdles and the hesitation of my family, I felt God literally ordering my steps to go. I found myself at an Amish farm turned bed-and-breakfast, staying in a room named El Roi—"The God Who Sees Me." Over my bed hung a picture of the woman at the well. The divine orchestration was undeniable. I was surrounded by "prayer warriors," including the host I call my "Little Giant in the Word"—a woman whose spiritual stature far exceeded her physical height.

On our first full day, I received a text from a colleague at the school where I work, asking for prayer. My instinct was to handle it later, but the prayer leader at the retreat stopped me in my tracks. "When someone asks you to pray," she said, "you do it right then. You don't know what situation they're in."

We stopped and prayed immediately. It was only later that I learned the gravity of that moment: a child had drowned on a field trip that very day. The school was in agony. God wasn't asking me to pass the duty on; He had brought me to that specific place of prayer to stand in the gap.

The Layers of Divine Timing

1. **The Prompt:** A sudden text message during a dedicated spiritual retreat.

2. **The Action:** Immediate, intercessory prayer led by a seasoned warrior.

3. **The Revelation:** Discovering the tragedy afterward, realizing God had positioned me to provide spiritual cover before I even knew the "why."

That experience reinforced a hard lesson: when God tells you to do something, you do it. Period. Obedience is the prerequisite for discernment.

The High Cost of Disobedience

While the retreat was a high point of spiritual connection, I also had to face the consequences of my own "low" points of obedience. This past year, I struggled with slacking on the tasks God gave me. Much of it was due to health battles with lupus, but some of it was a quiet rebellion against situations at my church. I learned the hard way that you cannot wait for things to "go your way" before you decide to follow God's way.

This lack of discernment led to one of the most surreal experiences of my life: being detained for forty-eight hours in a youth detention center at the age of fifty-eight.

It started with a lapse in judgment. I had stopped taking my lupus medication, mistakenly believing I was "healing myself" without God actually telling me to stop the treatment. I was physically unwell and spiritually out of sync. On a day I was supposed to be fasting and boycotting "big box" stores as part of a ministry initiative, I went to Walmart anyway. I was tired, my mind was foggy, and the "Scan & Go" system became a trap. I made mistakes—scanning items twice, missing others—and ended up accused of a felony offense over a $502 error.

I knew I shouldn't have been out. I knew I wasn't feeling well. I call it disobedience, but God called it an opportunity for a different kind of ministry.

Ministry in the Midst of a "Mess-Up"

Even in a jail cell, God's "grace and mercy sandwich" was present. I was confused—why was a fifty-eight-year-old woman being held in a detention center meant for youth? But then I saw it: a small cross drawn in pen on the wall of my cell.

I spent those forty-eight hours ministering to young girls who had no one to share the Word with them. I met another woman, an ordained minister, who was also there under questionable circumstances. We realized that while we were "detained," we were actually "deployed."

> **Key Takeaway:** God's grace doesn't just fix our mistakes; it repurposes them. My disobedience led me to a place where I could be useful to people who are often forgotten by the church.

Finding the Connections

Looking back, I can see the connections I missed in the moment:

- **The Consecration Connection:** I had skipped the youth consecration service at my church a month prior. Now, I was literally sitting in a room with the youth, forced to focus on them.
- **The Legal Lesson:** The attorney fees and the classes I had to take afterward opened my eyes

to the systemic issues of how people are wrongfully accused and how "big box" corporations operate.

- **The Testimony:** What could have been an embarrassing secret became a story of God's protection. The fine was minimal, the record was expunged, but the spiritual insight was permanent.

Cultivating Daily Discernment

Discernment isn't like riding a bike; you don't just learn it once and move on. It is a work in progress that requires daily maintenance. Even now, thoughts cross my mind and I start to second-guess. When those doubts creep in, I've learned to ask: "God, where are You in this picture?"

What feels "beneficial" or "advantageous" for me is rarely the same as God's plan. True discernment often leads to tough decisions that don't make sense to the world—or even to your own family. To practice this in your own life, I suggest the following:

- **Meditate and Pray:** Don't just talk to God; listen for the direction.

- **Search the Scriptures:** Look for the historical patterns. Human nature hasn't changed; someone in the Bible has navigated the exact "mess" you are currently in.

- **Wait for the "Sleep On It" Clarity:** If you aren't sure, ask God to show you in the stillness of the night.

A Living Testimony

God speaks through layered moments. He takes the text message from a friend, the mistake at a checkout counter, and the silence of a jail cell, and He weaves them into a testimony. We call them "mess-ups" or "wrong turns," but more often than not, they are God's way of moving us out of the path of an "accident" we couldn't see coming, or placing us in the path of someone who needs our light.

Stop, re-evaluate, and look at what was happening just before your "crisis" hit. You'll see the hands of God working. Your life is not a series of accidents; it is a living testimony of His orchestration.

Chapter 8:

The Ministry of Working

We often spend our lives chasing a vision of success that we've carefully curated—a specific career path, a certain level of education, or a dream home built from the ground up. We convince ourselves that these milestones define our worth and fulfill our purpose. However, I have learned through years of transition and trial that what we consider our life's calling may not be what God has planned for us at all. What we pictured as a "career" or "making a living" is often just the scaffolding for the real work God wants to do through us.

This chapter is about the ministry of working: the realization that physical labor, caretaking, and community service are not just chores or ways to pass the time, but are the very tools God uses for our spiritual restoration. When we shift our focus from what we can acquire to how we can serve, we find a fulfillment that money and titles could never provide.

Redefining Success and Value

For decades, I followed the traditional path. I did the schooling, earned the degrees, and put in the work. I thought my impact would come through medicine or medical research—finding cures that would change the world. In my mind, that was a "worthy" calling. Like many, I lived in a world that equated value with material things: cars, houses, and the ability to sustain a commercialized lifestyle.

I didn't realize how much I had tied my identity to those things until I was knocked down by a forced early retirement. Suddenly, the degrees and the status were gone. I was left asking, "Now what?" That question sent me into a deep depression. I felt like I had been sidelined before I was finished.

But looking back, I see that God was redirecting me. He allowed my loans to be forgiven and provided lump sums of money right when I thought I had nothing. Because I wasn't driven by money, I often gave it away to satisfy those around me who equated wealth with happiness. But God was teaching me that my value wasn't in my bank account or my title; it was in my willingness to be used.

The Shift to Caretaking and Community

My "ministry of what's next" began when I stopped looking at the global stage and started looking at the people right in front of me. It started with my mother.

Moving her to Georgia and becoming her primary caretaker was the first step in a new kind of labor.

Even while I was still working full-time opening a new school, having my mother and aunts visit and seeing the pride in their eyes gave me a sense of satisfaction that professional accolades never did. Eventually, that service expanded into my community through Delta Sigma Theta Sorority Inc.(shout out to my Linesisters) Whether it was working with the "Delta Dears", attending Nationals, Regional Seminars or just visiting headquarters in D.C. to learn how to get involved in local politics, I realized that as long as I was taking care of someone, I was okay.

This transition from medical researcher to caretaker wasn't a "step down." It was a restoration. I found myself:

- Opening "Ms. Angie's School" to care for and tutor children.
- Stepping in to handle funerals for neighbors when their own families couldn't.
- Managing doctor visits and daily care for my "Soror Mama."
- Living in the "Sandwich Generation," caring for my grandchildren and my mother simultaneously.

I am now living the life my sister, Sissy, and I used to dream about—a life centered on the Lifelong Learning Foundation. Helping others has become my life's work, and the fulfillment I get from it is far deeper than any "dream job" I once imagined.

Internal Restoration Through External Service

There is a profound connection between healing and helping. For a long time, I was the one who needed help. I was experimenting with over-the-counter medications just to numb the physical pain I was in, effectively making myself a "guinea pig" and phasing myself out of a useful life.

God restored my body and mind so that I could be the pilot for a change, not just the passenger. He allowed me to live many many times when I should not have. I found a professional, Dr. Mac, who was not just willing to listen to my complaints but was empathetic to my not wanting all the labels that come from those who depend on pain medications for a reasonable quality of life. With his help and God's Grace and Mercy my pain went to manageable levels so that I could get back out into the world. But the restoration wasn't just physical; it was legal and spiritual too. For a year, I carried the weight of a legal misunderstanding over my head, but God cleared that path, moving me from probation to freedom.

When you are restored, you have a responsibility to use that strength for others. I went from being someone who had to be driven to the doctor to being the one who drives others.

How to Serve Where You Are

You might feel that your "handicap"—whether it's physical pain, emotional trauma, or a complicated past—disqualifies you from ministry. I'm here to tell you to let that handicap empower you. Whatever it takes to get you to the starting line, do it, and then get involved.

- **Start Small:** If you can't do the "big" things, do the small things. Help one person a day.
- **Use Your Natural Talents:** If you can sing, sing. If you can cook, make a meal for a neighbor.
- **Simple Acts of Kindness:** Mow a lawn for someone with a broken leg, take in a neighbor's trash can, or shovel a walkway.
- **The Power of Presence:** Sometimes, just a smile and a hug can complete someone's day. You have no idea the impact a simple greeting can have on a person who feels invisible.

Pushing Through the Empty Cup

Sometimes, doing the work of ministry feels thankless. You may feel unappreciated by your inner circle, or like you are pouring from an empty cup. When those moments come, I've learned to "steal away" to God through journaling, prayer, and the Word.

I look to the life of Jesus as my blueprint: He kept on helping and kept on pushing through, regardless of how He felt or how He was treated. We may not see the rewards of our labor immediately—they are often "invisible rewards"—but the work is making a difference. Helping someone else makes you realize that no matter how bad you feel, you are still in a position to be a blessing. That realization is where your own healing truly begins.

Chapter 9:

The Restoration Is Here

Restoration is not a destination you reach and then unpack your bags; it is a profound emotional and spiritual turning point where the weight of the past finally gives way to the lightness of surrender. For so long, I was off-track, moving through a fog of physical pain and the crushing pressure of being a people-pleaser. I was "broken" in ways I couldn't even articulate to my inner circle. This chapter is about that moment the "whoosh" occurred—the moment I realized that God wasn't just working on me, but was ready to work through me. It is the story of how I moved from hiding my flaws behind a cocktail of medications to standing in the sunshine of His grace, finally free to say, "I am being restored."

The Card I Didn't Know I Needed

My journey into this breakthrough began at a retreat in Ohio. We were in our very first sit-down session, an intimate gathering where we were asked to pull a card from a deck. Rachel, the organizer, had bought these cards at the last minute because she'd lost her original icebreaker games. She didn't even know what was on them; she thought they were just blank index cards for us to write on.

When I pulled my card, it looked blank to me at first. But when I turned it over, there was one word that felt like a bolt of lightning: Restoration.

Underneath that word was Psalm 66:8-15. I read it then, and I kept reading it on my way back to where I was staying. The words pierced through the noise of my life:

"You have tested us, oh God. You have purified us like silver... We went through fire and flood, but You brought us to a place of great abundance."

I had been hearing the song "I've Been Restored" by Tasha Cobbs on repeat for weeks. I knew God had been working with me, but I didn't know the specifics of what I was asking for. I just knew I was tired of disappointing the people around me—one of my biggest pet peeves. I was hiding my flaws from the world, using over-the-counter meds to supplement my prescriptions because the pain was just too much. I was out of order.

When I read that Psalm, I realized that the "fire and flood" were behind me. God was bringing me back to a place of independence. I didn't want to have to depend on everyone else to finance my life or carry my burdens. I broke down into tears right there. I felt a relief so deep it was like a physical weight leaving my chest. In that room full of strangers who felt like sisters, I realized I wasn't the only one dealing with things I couldn't explain. I told my story, and I realized: if ten people in this small room are struggling with this, the whole world needs to hear that restoration is possible.

From People-Pleasing to Peace

Before this moment, I was a classic people-pleaser. I wanted everyone to be happy and comfortable, but I didn't realize that in doing so, I was letting everyone else dump their "stuff" into me. I was a vessel for everyone else's problems, and it left me shattered. I was "broken"—that is the only word for it. I was too weak to provide everything for everybody, yet I kept trying until my body and spirit gave out.

Restoration arrived when I finally understood that I don't have to be superhuman. My lupus doctor and my psychiatrist had been trying to tell me that for years, but I was too stubborn—too OCD—to hear it. I was mourning the loss of my career and my health. But at that retreat, when Sister Delphine held me in her arms, I learned that a hug can say more than a thousand words. She held me until I stopped crying and simply whispered, "It's okay. The spirit has already said it all."

That moment changed my perspective on my own role in my family. I have what I call my "8 Grammy Awards"—my eight grandchildren. The number eight signifies a new beginning, and that is exactly what they represent to me. I don't want to be the "perfect" Grammy who hides her pain anymore. I want to be their friend and their guide. I want them to see that I'm a God's "Grace and Mercy sandwich"—someone who has messed up, been restored, and is now walking in wisdom trying to learn daily.

Signs That Your Restoration Has Arrived

How do you know when the shift has happened? For me, it looked like this:

1. **A Lightbulb Moment:** You suddenly feel different. You realize you are no longer sinking into a hole of self-medication or despair.

2. **The "Enemy" Gets Busy:** Ironically, when you start to grow, people around you might start saying things that aren't compliments. They might call you names because they don't recognize the new, stronger version of you. Don't stop. That pushback is often the first sign that you're actually changing.

3. **A Shift in Thought:** You start to care less about what the "next person" thinks and more about what God has planned.

4. **The Desire to Help Others:** You move from a pity party to a "purpose party." You get out of bed, even when you don't feel 100%, because someone else needs a ride to the doctor or a kind word.

Tools for the Journey: Music and Letters

Restoration is a work in progress; it's not a one-and-done event. There are still days I want to pull the covers over my head because I feel judged or unwell. In those moments, I use my "tools."

I found that I couldn't always voice my hurt out loud without wanting to hurt someone back, which isn't in my nature. So, I started writing letters. Even if I never mail them, writing the words down frees me from the hurt. It defends my spirit without creating more conflict.

The other tool is music. During the pandemic, when I was waiting five days for surgery on a leg that was literally broken in half, no medication could touch that pain. I lived with my earpiece , listening to gospel music 24/7 to block out the noise and the negativity. One song in particularly called "You Know My Name" by Tasha Cobbs became my comfort confirmational song. It would remind me that no matter what God knows who I am.

The Significance of a Name

That song, "You Know My Name," is deeply personal to me. Believe it or not, I didn't have a legal name for the first dozen or so months of my life. My parents just called me "Baby Martin" on my medical records until the county forced them to name me. They eventually chose Angie, short for Angela except my parents used only (Angie no middle name Martin), which means

“Angel." It’s ironic because my family sometimes criticizes me for being a nurturer and "watching over" everyone, but they are the ones who gave me a name that means "messenger" or "guardian." It taught me that God knew my name even when the state of Illinois didn't. He is my El Roi—the God who sees me.

Walking Forward in Faith

If you remember nothing else about my story, remember this: Angie lives. I am a person who has gone through the fire and come out willing to talk about it. If you’ve never been through anything, you have nothing to share. My "messes" became my ministry.

I am still a work in progress. I’m still finding my place in this world, and I’m still learning to be content even when my living situation isn't exactly where I want it to be. But I am moving forward with unwavering faith.

To my readers who are seeking their own restoration, I offer this daily move:

- **Acknowledge the Brokenness:** Ask yourself, "Where are my broken spots?" You can't be restored from something you won't name.
- **Practice Quiet Time:** Get into your quiet spaces and listen. God speaks in the silence.
- **Put God First:** Set the stage of your life with Him at the center. It’s the only way to have a truly happy, restored life.

- **Accept the "Delay":** Remember that a delay is not a denial. It is often a period of preparation for something bigger and better.

I dedicate this journey to my son, who has been my "stone" here on earth. He gives me the courage to keep going and the honesty to tell me when I'm messing up. With God leading me and my family beside me, I know that this is just Part One of the restoration. The best is yet to come.

www.ingramcontent.com/pod-product-compliance
Lightning Source LLC
LaVergne TN
LVHW090537110826
845146LV00003B/1141

9798218939557